SP★RTS
IN ACTION

Martial Arts
in Action

功夫 功夫

Heather Levigne
Illustrated by Bonna Rouse
Crabtree Publishing Company
www.crabtreebooks.com

Created by Bobbie Kalman

For John Evoy,
who believes in magic

Editor-in-Chief
Bobbie Kalman

Author
Heather Levigne

Managing editor
Lynda Hale

Editors
Kate Calder
Hannelore Sotzek
Niki Walker

Computer design
Lynda Hale

Photo researchers
Heather Levigne
Heather Fitzpatrick

Production coordinator
Hannelore Sotzek

Illustrations
Bonna Rouse

Special thanks to
John Siemens, Mario Quiquero, Steven Falconer, Aleksandar Balta, Jesse Bloys,
Matthew Boudreau, Christopher Bryjak, Michael Burke, Alfonso Carlone, Samantha
Carlone, Tyler Caughill, David Cushman, Ross DeCaria, Aleksandar Djermanovic,
Tatjana Djermanovic, Christian Duggan, Sarah Duggan, Rhys Etherington, Josh Evans,
Meg Evans, Eric Frost, Jason Frost, Andrea Giacometti, Dale Giacometti, Robert
Giacometti (cover model), Michael Hipwell, Damin Kaine, Josh Malekzadeh,
Mitchell Mountain, Travis Nan, Domenic Olivo, Rebecca Olivo, Kyle Punch,
Christine Quiquero, Alexis Robinson, Michael Szoke, Billy Szolga, Harmony Szolga,
Kenneth Webster

Consultant
Mario Quiquero, 6th *dan*, Seido Kan Karate School, Niagara Falls

Photographs
All photographs by Marc Crabtree except the following: Amwell/Stone: page 24;
Chris Cole/Stone: page 28; Digital Stock: back cover; Mark Downey/Lucid Images:
title page, pages 5, 26, 29, 31; Philip Lee Harvey/Stone: page 25; Milt & Joan Mann,
Cameramann Int'l: page 9 (bottom); SportsChrome: page 18; Elias Wakan/Pacific
Rim Slide Bank: page 23

Digital prepress
Embassy Graphics

空手 功夫 太極拳 空手 功夫 太極拳 空手 功夫 太極拳 空手

Crabtree Publishing Company

www.crabtreebooks.com   1-800-387-7650

PMB 16A
350 Fifth Avenue,
Suite 3308
New York, NY
10118

612 Welland Avenue
St. Catharines,
Ontario
Canada
L2M 5V6

73 Lime Walk
Headington,
Oxford
OX3 7AD
United Kingdom

Cataloging-in-Publication Data
Levigne, Heather
  Martial arts in action

p. cm. — (Sports in action)
Includes index.

ISBN 0-7787-0169-7 (library bound) — ISBN 0-7787-0181-6 (pbk.)
This book introduces various martial arts styles, including karate,
judo, tae kwon do, kung fu, and aikido.

1. Martial arts—Juvenile literature. [1.Martial arts.] I. Rouse, Bonna, ill.
II. Title. III. Series: Kalman, Bobbie. Sports in action.

GV1101.35 .L48 2001   j796.8—dc21   LC 00-060390
                                                          CIP

Contents

空手 太極拳

태권도

人体 What are Martial Arts?

Martial arts are methods of **combat**, or fighting, that began in Asian countries such as Japan, China, and Korea. Even though martial arts are based on fighting skills, they are used only for self-defense. Students of martial arts do not use their skills to attack or harm others unless they are attacked first.

This student is performing a powerful kick. The aim of martial arts is to teach your mind and body to work together.

*Karate students often use a **bo**, which is a long staff, to practice their techniques.*

Many types

There are many types of martial arts, and they are all are based on similar movements. Most include fighting moves such as kicking, punching, throwing, and **blocking**. For some martial arts, students use weapons such as bows or swords. Aikido, wu shu, and tai chi use only gentle, flowing movements. They are less aggressive than other types of martial arts.

Learning for different reasons

Today, people all over the world practice martial arts. Many people learn for self-defense. Some want to develop self-discipline and a strong mind. Others enjoy martial arts because they are good forms of exercise.

Practice makes perfect

Becoming an expert in a martial art takes dedication and many years of practice. Competitions provide an opportunity for students to fine-tune their techniques and become more advanced. In martial arts, however, winning is not as important as achieving your personal best. Even the experts continue to learn new moves and improve their skills.

Gentle sports

Although many martial arts include punching, kicking, and throwing opponents, the risk of getting injured is low. Students learn how to **spar**, or fight without hurting one another. When punching and kicking, they pull back each movement so that they do not strike their opponent. The object of sparring is to improve your fighting skills. Be careful not to hurt your opponent.

In China, tai chi is a popular martial art. Many people of all ages practice outdoors so they can enjoy fresh air while they exercise.

The beginning of martial arts

Thousands of years ago, an Indian priest and knight named Bodhidharma brought a religion called **Zen Buddhism** to China along with a series of exercises. People studied the religion and practiced the exercises to help strengthen their mind and body. Over time, these exercises changed into a form of combat. By the 1100s, Bodhidharma's teachings had spread to Japan, where they evolved into many different forms of combat.

# In the *Dojo*

Most martial arts are practiced inside a training hall called a *dojo*. *Dojo* is a Japanese word meaning "school." Kung fu students call their school a *kwoon*, and students of tae kwon do learn in a *dojang*. If you want to study at a martial arts school, you first have to decide which art you want to learn. Make a list of the schools in your area and visit each one to watch the classes. After a class is finished, talk to the instructor and ask questions to help you decide if that school and martial art are right for you.

Teachers

Most martial arts instructors are patient and helpful. They spend time working with each student and make sure that everyone learns at his or her own pace. In return for their efforts, they expect students to pay attention, practice, and work hard. Instructors of each martial art have different names, but all the names have the same meaning, which is "teacher" or "respected elder." A karate teacher is called *sensei*. A tae kwon do teacher is *sabumnim*, and kung fu students call their teacher *sifu*.

Respect

Respect is a very important part of martial arts. Students must show respect for their teachers, parents, and other students. When entering and leaving the training area, students bow to show respect to one another. They always speak quietly and obey the rules of their training hall.

At the beginning and end of each lesson, the students and the sensei *bow to one another.*

Students who are not sparring wait their turn quietly. They kneel in the **seiza** position by sitting back on their heels and placing their hands on their thighs.

Mirrors on the walls allow students to see themselves and perform their movements correctly.

Students should not whisper or talk while the instructor is speaking.

Participants may not wear shoes on the tatami.

The floor of a traditional **dojo** is covered with woven straw mats called **tatami**. Most modern dojos have smooth wooden or tiled floors.

Each **dojo** has rules that students must obey. At some schools, the students help keep the training area clean to honor their environment.

7

人体 Dressing for Martial Arts 人体

Beginners in martial arts need to wear only loose, comfortable clothing such as sweatpants and a T-shirt. If you are planning to study martial arts for a long time or enter competitions, you will need a proper uniform. To prevent injuries, some students wear protective equipment such as mouth guards, helmets, gloves, and shin or elbow pads.

Your appearance should always be clean and neat. If your hair is long, keep it tied back. Your fingernails should be short and well-groomed. Most martial arts involve close contact with other students, so remove any jewelry to avoid hurting yourself or others.

The *gi*

Most martial arts students wear loose-fitting cotton pants and a top called a *gi*. The *gi* is usually white or black. Some have decorative stripes on the sides of the pants or along the arms. Special uniforms with the logo of the *dojo* are often worn for competitions. Some students wear a plain white T-shirt underneath. A long belt, or *obi*, is tied around the waist to secure the *gi*. Martial arts students do not wear socks or shoes—they practice in bare feet. In tae kwon do the uniform is called the *dobok*. It is important to keep your uniform clean and tidy. Dirty, wrinkled clothes show a lack of respect.

Kung fu

Kung fu students wear black pants and a shirt. The shirt is held closed with several clasps instead of an *obi*. A colored sash is worn around the waist, to show the student's skill level. The broadsword, shown left, is a traditional kung fu weapon.

mune
(upper body protector)

men
(head guard)

do *(chest protector)*

Kendo

Kendo is an ancient Japanese martial art. Its name means "the way of the sword." Competitors use wooden or bamboo swords called **shinai**. They wear padded equipment to prevent injuries. When getting dressed, students sit on the floor with their gear next to them. They must put on each piece of equipment in the correct order.

kote *(gloves)*

tare *(hip protector)*

hakama *(divided skirt)*

Belts of many colors

As students become more skilled, they earn different colored belts. Beginners wear a white belt, which signifies no rank at all. Students must pass tests to show that they are ready to move to a higher rank. The beginning levels are called **kyus**. Students progress from white belt to first *kyu*, or brown belt. The next level is first **dan**, or black belt. In most belt systems, there are ten levels of black belt. It takes most students about five years to reach the first black-belt level.

black belt (first dan*)*

brown belt (first kyu*)*

blue belt (second kyu*)*

green belt (third kyu*)*

orange belt (fourth kyu*)*

yellow belt (fifth kyu*)*

white belt (no rank)

Warming Up

Before attempting any of the techniques shown in this book, it is important to warm up your muscles. Stretching helps prevent injuries and keeps your body limber.

The rack

Kneel on your hands and knees. Spread apart your knees as wide as you can. Slowly "walk" forward and backward on your hands. Hold this stretch for 30 seconds.

Front splits

When doing splits, do not force the stretch—extend your legs only as far as feels comfortable. Slowly ease into the splits by extending one leg in front of your body and the other one behind you. Make sure the instep of your back foot is on the floor. Hold this position for 20 seconds.

Push-ups

Lie on your stomach. Place your hands flat on the floor beneath your shoulders. Push yourself up using your arms. Be sure to keep your back flat. Repeat ten times. Try doing push-ups in a kneeling position if you find them too difficult with your legs extended.

Crunch V-sit

Sit with your legs stretched out and your hands behind your head. Raise your legs toward your chest and bring your upper body forward to meet them. Do ten crunches.

Canoe stretches

Sit on the floor facing your partner, with the soles of your feet touching. Lean forward and grab your partner's hands. Gently pull your partner forward until his or her nose touches his or her knees, or as far as feels comfortable. Take turns repeating the stretch ten times.

Toe touches

Stand with your legs wide apart. Bend and touch your left toes with your right hand, and then touch your right toes with your left hand. Repeat ten times. Do not straighten up between toe touches.

Meditation

Many martial arts students **meditate** before they practice. They sit quietly and concentrate on breathing. Meditation helps them clear their mind so they can focus on performing their moves. They learn to ignore distractions and pay attention to the instructor. Some students meditate on the floor in a sitting or kneeling position. Others stand with their arms at their sides.

人体 Basic Moves 人体

Since all martial arts are based on the same ancient fighting system, there are similarities among them. Students of every martial art learn a basic **defensive stance** from which all other movements come. Most martial arts also include some form of punching, blocking, and kicking. Once you learn how to perform these basic moves, you can move on to more advanced techniques.

The basic punch

When punching, it is important to make a proper fist so you do not hurt your fingers or wrists. Curl your fingers toward your palm and place your thumb over your fingers. Never curl your fingers around your thumb—it could get broken! Keep your knuckles level with your arm to add strength to your punch.

To make a **forward punch**, start by holding out your right fist with your palm facing down. Keep your left fist close to your body at waist level and facing up. Pull in your right fist and punch out with your left fist. Step forward with your left foot at the same time. Twist your fists so that the left palm now faces down and the right one faces up. When punching, hold your back straight and keep your elbows close to your body. Do not turn your shoulders.

The basic stance

Your stance is a combination of the position of your feet and hands, the distribution of your weight, and the position of your body opposite your opponent. For a basic stance, stand with your feet shoulder-width apart. Hold your fists slightly in front of your chest and look straight ahead. Keep your back straight, but not stiff. You should feel focused and relaxed.

Now that these karate students are positioned in a basic stance, they are ready to spar.

The basic block

A block stops an opponent's punch or kick before it hits your body. The type of block you use depends on where your opponent is aiming. In this picture, the boy with the white belt is delivering a kick to the lower body of the boy with the yellow belt. To block the kick, the second boy steps forward with his right foot and moves his right arm downward. He keeps his other arm ready to block his upper body from another strike.

*This girl is delivering a **leg sweep** to her opponent. She kicks his foot out from under him to throw him off-balance...*

Falling down

One of the most important skills you must learn is how to hit the ground safely. If you do not fall properly, you can get injured during a sparring match. Use a mat to practice falling. Squat down and hold both arms in front of your body. Be sure to keep your body relaxed. Allow yourself to fall gently to one side. Kick out with your right foot and slap the floor with your right hand. Place your left hand under your head to protect it.

The basic kick

Kicks are more powerful than punches because the muscles in your legs are larger and stronger than the muscles in your arms. The **front kick** is one of the first ones you will learn in a martial art such as karate or tae kwon do. Begin by standing with your left leg forward and your fists up in front of your body. Bring your right knee up and kick out, extending your leg toward your target. Remember to pull back your toes and strike with the ball of your foot—you could hurt your toes if you use them to kick your target.

...and down he goes! He breaks his fall with his free arm and leg.

空手 Karate 空手

Karate is one of the most popular Japanese martial arts. There are four major styles of karate—*wado ryu*, *shito ryu*, *goju ryu*, and *shotokan*. Each type uses techniques such as punching, striking, and kicking.

Katas

Students use **katas** to practice and perfect their karate techniques without sparring. A *kata* is a series of blocks, punches, strikes, and kicks performed in a pattern. Do not rush when doing *katas*—precision is more important than speed in these exercises. As you become more advanced, the *katas* you must learn will become more difficult.

Karate students often practice kicking using a padded target.

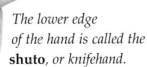

The lower edge of the hand is called the **shuto**, *or knifehand.*

Karate weapons

Karate means "empty hand," which refers to the lack of weapons used for most karate styles and movements. Several types, however, use weapons as part of the training, such as the *bo* and the *tonfa*, which looks like the side-handled baton used by some police officers.

(right) This instructor is demonstrating **escrima**, *which is the art of using a baton.*

Down he goes!

To take down an opponent, use a **counterbalancing** move. In this set of pictures, the girl is defending herself against a strike from the boy.

1. The boy steps toward the girl and throws a punch. She raises her arm to block his attack.

2. The girl steps forward and places her leg behind his. At the same time, she grabs his shirt with her free hand.

3. While holding him firmly, she pushes her opponent backward over her leg.

4. This move causes him to lose his balance and fall to the floor.

17

*For a **back kick**, extend your leg straight out behind your body.*

태 권 도 Tae kwon do 태 권 도

Tae kwon do is a Korean martial art. Its name means "the way of the foot and fist." This powerful martial art is similar to karate, but it places more emphasis on kicking. Tae kwon do is the national sport of Korea. It is also an Olympic sport.

Just for kicks

Tae kwon do uses more kicks than any other martial art. Students learn how to use various parts of their feet for different kicks. For example, when performing a **front snap kick**, the toes are pulled back and the ball of the foot is used to strike the opponent. For a **turning kick**, the toes are pointed and the top of the foot is used for striking.

The poomse

Like a *kata* in karate, a ***poomse*** is a series of movements that students practice in order to improve their technique. When doing a *poomse*, students imagine they are striking an opponent so they perform each kick and punch forcefully.

While kicking her opponent, this tae kwon do student holds her arm across her body to block his attack.

Shout it out!

When doing powerful moves such as front kicks and punches, let out a loud yell, or *kihap*. Yelling helps tighten your stomach muscles, which protects you from getting your wind knocked out if your opponent strikes you. Shouting also startles your opponent and allows you to catch him or her off guard. Concentrate on yelling from your stomach rather than forcing it from your throat.

Jumping front kick

A move that gets you off the ground, such as a **jumping kick**, is referred to as a **flying technique**.

1. To kick with your left leg, jump up off your left foot.

2. As you land on your right foot, raise your left foot.

3. Kick out with your left leg. Be sure to extend it completely.

Kung fu

Over five thousand years ago, the Shaolin monks of China developed a system of fighting to defend their monastery from thieves. Their fighting style became known as kung fu, which means "sustained effort or skill." Later, the monks taught their skills to other people in the village, and kung fu began to spread throughout China.

Study hard

Most styles of kung fu are made up of fast, short strikes and blocks. Students practice for many years to develop quick reflexes. They study three things—*tse*, or mental ability; *tee*, or physical ability; and *dar*, or character.

Hard and soft kung fu

There are hundreds of styles of kung fu. Some experts divide them into two main groups—hard and soft. The hard style is strong and forceful. Students use more power when striking and kicking. Soft kung fu uses fewer aggressive movements than hard kung fu. Students use strength to unbalance their opponents rather than strike them.

The animal stances

Some styles of kung fu are named for animals that are important in Chinese culture, such as the dragon, tiger, and crane. Other styles include the horse, praying mantis, leopard, snake, and monkey. The movements used for each style imitate those of the animal for which it is named.

The dragon style of kung fu is powerful. Students use strong, direct attacks on their opponents.

The wing chun punch

The basic punch used in kung fu is the **wing chun punch**. It is a short, fast strike that allows you to deliver a lot of power without using a lot of energy. A fast punch such as this one is effective because it is difficult for an opponent to block.

1. Bend your elbow and open your hand. Point your fingers toward your target and bend your thumb.

2. Straighten your arm and curl in your fingers toward the palm of your hand.

3. Clench your fist and extend your arm toward your target. Make sure your thumb is outside your fingers.

The tiger technique is made up of slashing and clubbing hand movements.

The crane style uses skillful footwork to avoid opponents. The hands are used to "peck" at them.

柔術 Jujitsu 柔術

Jujitsu is one of the oldest martial arts that is practiced today. Its name means "gentle art," but it is not very gentle! Jujitsu students learn how to use their opponents' strength against them. They use throwing, holding, and **grappling**, or wrestling, techniques to cause their opponents to lose their balance.

Watch that elbow!

A punch is not the only strike you can make with your arm. In this sequence of moves, the girl is demonstrating an **elbow strike**.

1. The students begin in the defensive stance.
2. The girl then steps forward and quickly brings up her elbow toward her opponent's face.

The samurai

Thousands of years ago, Japanese warriors known as *samurai* practiced a deadly form of jujitsu. They were soldiers of the *daimyo*, who were the landowners in control of areas of Japan. Protecting the *daimyo* was considered the highest honor for a *samurai* warrior. The *samurai* followed a code called *bushido*, which means "the way of the samurai." Through *bushido*, the *samurai* learned about loyalty, self-control, and noble behavior. They were extremely proud of their training in martial arts.

*The **s**amurai were a **mounted** army, which means they fought on horseback. They carried a sword or a bow and arrows to defend themselves. Most fought alone or in small groups.*

Locked up

Jujitsu students use techniques that **immobilize** their opponents, or stop them from moving. The technique shown here is called an **arm lock**.

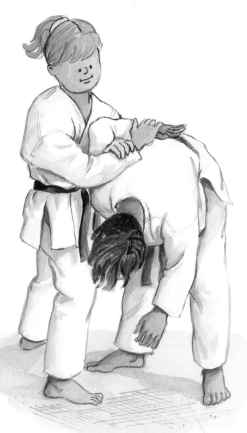

1. The girl takes hold of the other student's elbow with her right hand. She holds his hand with her left hand.

2. She bends his arm over her hand, "locking" it behind his back. He cannot free his arm from this position.

柔道 **Judo** 柔道

Like jujitsu, judo uses grappling techniques to defeat opponents. In a judo match, points are scored for throwing an opponent onto the mat. Students also win points for pinning their opponents to the mat and for applying pressure to their arm joints or neck.

*Judo means "gentle way." In this Japanese martial art, students do not use direct attacks to overcome their opponents. Instead, they learn to use **leverage**, or balance, to gain control over their opponents.*

Using leverage

In judo, you will learn how to use leverage to unbalance your opponents. Use the strength and force of your opponent's attack to throw him or her to the mat. For example, if you pull on an opponent's pushing movement, he or she will become unbalanced. Then you will be able to throw him or her easily to the floor. Once your opponent is on the mat, you can use **holds** and **locks** to restrain him or her.

Falling properly is very important in judo because most of the techniques involve throwing an opponent down onto the mat—and being thrown yourself!

合気道 **Aikido** 合気道

Aikido is a gentle Japanese martial art. Students do not use punching, striking, or kicking techniques. Instead, they throw their opponents off-balance using smooth, flowing movements. The word aikido means "way of harmony." There are few competitions in aikido because students, called *aikidoka*, do not use any **offensive**, or attacking, movements. All aikido movements are defensive.

The importance of ki

Part of the word "aikido" is *ki*, which means "energy." *Aikidoka* believe that energy in the body begins in the abdomen. It then travels throughout the body from this area. Learning how to concentrate on your *ki* and use it properly takes practice.

Aikido students wear a wide, split skirt called a **hakama**.

Preparing a block

Students of aikido closely watch their opponents' movements so they can determine what they will do next. Knowing whether an opponent is going to kick or strike helps *aikidoka* prepare the proper type of block. For example, if your opponent raises a leg to kick you, get ready to grab it and raise it higher. This move will unbalance your opponent.

(right) This instructor is showing how to deflect a kick. He uses his arm to catch the student's leg and then turns his body around to knock the student off-balance.

Putting on the pressure

Aikidoka learn how to put pressure on sensitive parts of their opponents' body such as the wrists, elbows, and shoulders. An aikido instructor teaches the proper way to use these techniques. They can be harmful if they are not used carefully. In this picture, a student is immobilizing his opponent by turning and holding his wrist.

Be very gentle when practicing techniques in which pressure is applied to the body.

More Martial Arts

There are hundreds of styles of martial arts. Karate, kung fu, judo, and tae kwon do are the most popular styles studied in North America. Other styles are popular in countries such as Thailand, Brazil, and India.

Sumo wrestling

Sumo wrestling is a popular spectator sport in Japan. Matches are held inside a ring. To win, sumo wrestlers, or *sumatori*, must push their opponents out of the ring or force them to touch the ground with a part of their body other than the soles of their feet. *Sumatori* use their huge bodies to push, trip, throw, and slap their opponents to the mat.

Tai chi

Tai chi, which means "great ultimate fist," is a Chinese martial art. It is based on an ancient fighting system that used strikes and blows with the hands and feet. Today, the graceful movements of tai chi are not used for fighting. Instead, people practice this martial art as a gentle form of relaxation and exercise.

Tai chi incorporates deep breathing, good posture, and a firmly rooted stance into the movements.

(opposite page) Before each match, sumatori *perform a ring-entering ritual that includes clapping their hands and raising th arms into the air. Stomping the feet on the floor during this ritual is believed to scare away bad spirits.*

Wu shu

Wu shu is a Chinese word that means "martial arts." Wu shu is one of the gentlest martial arts. Students practice flowing, dancelike movements. They must be flexible in order to leap, roll, and stretch. Sometimes the movements are performed with music. Wu shu students also use traditional weapons such as spears.

Muay thai

Muay thai is also called Thai boxing or kickboxing. This aggressive martial art is the national sport of Thailand. Thai children begin learning muay thai at a very young age. The techniques are similar to those of boxing in North America. Competitors wear boxing gloves and full-body contact is allowed.

Kendo

Kendo is one of the most popular martial arts studied in Japan. Kendo competitors called *kendoka* use wooden or bamboo swords called *shinai* and wear padded equipment to protect themselves from injuries. Each kendo bout, or match, lasts less than five minutes. To win, a student must score two points. Students score points by touching eight different spots on their opponent's body with their sword: the left or right side of the head; the top of the head; the left or right side of the body; each of the wrists; and the throat. The attacker must call out the name of the spot when he or she touches it.

Capoeira

In the 1600's, African slaves in Brazil created a type of martial art called **capoeira**. Slave owners forbid the slaves to practice this art because they were afraid the slaves would become powerful. To practice their skills, the slaves disguised them as a type of acrobatic dance. Today, people practice capoeira using drums and other musical instruments.

*Kenpo, which means "fist law," is a Japanese martial art. This aggressive martial art combines punching and kicking movements from karate with holds and throws from jujitsu and judo. The student shown above is demonstrating kenpo techniques using a weapon called a **kama**.*

空手 功夫 太極拳 空手 功夫 太極拳 空手 功夫 太極拳 空手

Martial Arts Words

bo A long wooden staff used in karate

dan A high level of achievement used to rank the ability of black belt karate students

dojang A training room for tae kwon do students

gi A karate uniform

hakama A long, wide split skirt used in aikido

kata A series of punches, kicks, and blocks practiced by karate students

kihap A loud yell released while making powerful moves; also called *kiai*

kwoon A training room for kung fu students

kyu A lower level of achievement used to rank the ability of karate students

meditate To sit quietly and concentrate on spiritual matters

poomse A series of punches, kicks, and blocks practiced by tae kwon do students

sabumnim A tae kwon do teacher

samurai An ancient order of Japanese warriors

seiza A kneeling position held by students who are waiting their turn to spar

sensei A karate teacher

shuto The bottom edge of the hand

sifu A kung fu teacher

spar To fight for sport without intentionally hurting the other person

stance A position held to ready the body for a particular move

tatami A woven straw mat used to cover the floor of a *dojo*

tonfa A wood-handled baton used as a weapon in some types of karate

Zen Buddhism A religion from India upon which martial arts are based

Index

空手 功夫 太極拳 空手 功夫 太極拳 空手 功夫 太極拳 空手

1 2 3 4 5 6 7 8 9 0 Printed in the U.S.A. 9 8 7 6 5 4 3 2 1 0